50 Dairy-Free Desserts for Sweet Cravings

By: Kelly Johnson

Table of Contents

- Coconut Milk Rice Pudding
- Dairy-Free Chocolate Mousse
- Avocado Chocolate Pudding
- Vegan Coconut Macaroons
- Almond Flour Brownies
- Fruit Sorbet
- Chia Seed Pudding
- Coconut Whipped Cream
- Banana Oatmeal Cookies
- Vegan Chocolate Chip Cookies
- Dairy-Free Cheesecake
- Apple Crisp
- Peanut Butter Banana Ice Cream
- Cacao Nib Energy Bites
- Pumpkin Pie Bars
- Chocolate Avocado Brownies
- Peach Crumble
- Vegan Lemon Bars
- Date and Nut Energy Balls
- Dairy-Free Chocolate Cake
- Mango Coconut Sticky Rice
- Dairy-Free Chocolate Bark
- Lemon Coconut Macaroons
- Coconut Flour Pancakes
- Carrot Cake Muffins
- Dairy-Free Tiramisu
- Chocolate-Dipped Strawberries
- Banana Coconut Muffins
- Vegan Rice Crispy Treats
- Oatmeal Chocolate Chip Bars
- Raspberry Chia Seed Jam
- Coconut Panna Cotta
- Fruit Salad with Lime Dressing
- Vegan Snickerdoodles
- Chocolate Coconut Energy Bites

- Banana Split Bowl
- Lemon Coconut Bars
- Vegan Pumpkin Muffins
- Chocolate Chip Blondies
- Peanut Butter Cups
- Caramelized Pineapple
- Vegan Chocolate Chip Pancakes
- Almond Joy Bites
- Dairy-Free Key Lime Pie
- Coconut Crème Brûlée
- Chocolate Banana Bread
- Vegan Berry Parfait
- Dairy-Free Oatmeal Raisin Cookies
- Coconut Lime Pudding
- Chocolate Dipped Fruit

Coconut Milk Rice Pudding

Ingredients:

- 1 cup Arborio rice
- 4 cups coconut milk
- 1/2 cup sugar
- 1 tsp vanilla extract
- 1/2 tsp cinnamon
- Pinch of salt

Instructions:

1. In a saucepan, combine the rice, coconut milk, sugar, vanilla extract, cinnamon, and salt.
2. Bring to a gentle boil over medium heat, then reduce to low and simmer, stirring frequently, for about 30-35 minutes or until the rice is tender and the pudding thickens.
3. Remove from heat and let cool slightly before serving.

Dairy-Free Chocolate Mousse

Ingredients:

- 1 1/2 cups silken tofu, drained
- 1/2 cup dairy-free dark chocolate chips, melted
- 1/4 cup maple syrup
- 1 tsp vanilla extract

Instructions:

1. In a blender, combine silken tofu, melted chocolate, maple syrup, and vanilla extract.
2. Blend until smooth and creamy.
3. Spoon the mousse into serving dishes and refrigerate for at least 1 hour before serving.

Avocado Chocolate Pudding

Ingredients:

- 2 ripe avocados, peeled and pitted
- 1/4 cup cocoa powder
- 1/4 cup maple syrup
- 1/4 cup almond milk
- 1 tsp vanilla extract

Instructions:

1. In a food processor, combine avocados, cocoa powder, maple syrup, almond milk, and vanilla extract.
2. Blend until smooth and creamy.
3. Transfer to serving bowls and chill for 30 minutes before serving.

Vegan Coconut Macaroons

Ingredients:

- 3 cups shredded coconut
- 1/2 cup almond flour
- 1/2 cup maple syrup
- 1 tsp vanilla extract
- 1/4 tsp salt

Instructions:

1. Preheat the oven to 350°F (175°C) and line a baking sheet with parchment paper.
2. In a bowl, combine shredded coconut, almond flour, maple syrup, vanilla extract, and salt.
3. Drop spoonfuls of the mixture onto the prepared baking sheet and bake for 15-20 minutes until golden brown.
4. Let cool before serving.

Almond Flour Brownies

Ingredients:

- 1 cup almond flour
- 1/2 cup cocoa powder
- 1/2 cup maple syrup
- 1/4 cup coconut oil, melted
- 2 eggs (or flax eggs for vegan)
- 1 tsp vanilla extract
- 1/4 tsp salt

Instructions:

1. Preheat the oven to 350°F (175°C) and grease an 8x8-inch baking pan.
2. In a bowl, combine almond flour, cocoa powder, maple syrup, melted coconut oil, eggs, vanilla extract, and salt.
3. Pour the batter into the prepared pan and bake for 20-25 minutes.
4. Allow to cool before cutting into squares.

Fruit Sorbet

Ingredients:

- 2 cups fruit (mango, strawberry, or any preferred fruit), diced and frozen
- 1/4 cup maple syrup (adjust to taste)
- 1 tbsp lemon juice

Instructions:

1. In a food processor, combine the frozen fruit, maple syrup, and lemon juice.
2. Blend until smooth and creamy.
3. Serve immediately or freeze for a firmer texture.

Chia Seed Pudding

Ingredients:

- 1/4 cup chia seeds
- 1 cup almond milk (or any plant-based milk)
- 2 tbsp maple syrup
- 1/2 tsp vanilla extract

Instructions:

1. In a bowl, mix chia seeds, almond milk, maple syrup, and vanilla extract.
2. Stir well and let sit for 10 minutes, then stir again to prevent clumping.
3. Cover and refrigerate for at least 2 hours or overnight before serving.

Coconut Whipped Cream

Ingredients:

- 1 can (13.5 oz) full-fat coconut milk, refrigerated overnight
- 2 tbsp powdered sugar (or to taste)
- 1 tsp vanilla extract

Instructions:

1. Open the chilled can of coconut milk and scoop out the solid cream into a mixing bowl, discarding the liquid.
2. Using an electric mixer, beat the coconut cream until fluffy.
3. Add powdered sugar and vanilla extract, and continue to beat until well combined.
4. Serve immediately or refrigerate until ready to use.

Banana Oatmeal Cookies

Ingredients:

- 2 ripe bananas, mashed
- 1 cup rolled oats
- 1/2 cup almond flour
- 1/2 tsp cinnamon
- 1/4 cup chocolate chips (optional)

Instructions:

1. Preheat the oven to 350°F (175°C) and line a baking sheet with parchment paper.
2. In a bowl, mix together mashed bananas, rolled oats, almond flour, cinnamon, and chocolate chips (if using).
3. Drop spoonfuls of the mixture onto the prepared baking sheet and flatten slightly.
4. Bake for 10-12 minutes until golden brown. Let cool before serving.

Vegan Chocolate Chip Cookies

Ingredients:

- 1 cup almond flour
- 1/2 cup coconut flour
- 1/2 tsp baking soda
- 1/4 tsp salt
- 1/2 cup coconut oil, melted
- 1/2 cup maple syrup
- 1 tsp vanilla extract
- 1/2 cup dairy-free chocolate chips

Instructions:

1. Preheat the oven to 350°F (175°C) and line a baking sheet with parchment paper.
2. In a bowl, combine almond flour, coconut flour, baking soda, and salt.
3. In another bowl, mix melted coconut oil, maple syrup, and vanilla extract.
4. Combine wet and dry ingredients, then fold in chocolate chips.
5. Drop spoonfuls of dough onto the prepared baking sheet and bake for 10-12 minutes.

Dairy-Free Cheesecake

Ingredients:

- 2 cups cashews, soaked for 4 hours
- 1/2 cup coconut milk
- 1/2 cup maple syrup
- 1/4 cup coconut oil, melted
- 1 tsp vanilla extract
- 1/4 cup lemon juice
- 1 cup graham cracker crumbs (or almond flour for a gluten-free option)
- 1/4 cup coconut oil, melted (for crust)

Instructions:

1. In a food processor, combine soaked cashews, coconut milk, maple syrup, melted coconut oil, vanilla extract, and lemon juice. Blend until smooth.
2. In a separate bowl, mix graham cracker crumbs and melted coconut oil. Press into the bottom of a springform pan.
3. Pour the cheesecake filling over the crust and refrigerate for at least 4 hours until set.

Apple Crisp

Ingredients:

- 4 cups apples, peeled and sliced
- 1/2 cup oats
- 1/2 cup almond flour
- 1/2 cup brown sugar
- 1/4 cup coconut oil, melted
- 1 tsp cinnamon
- Pinch of salt

Instructions:

1. Preheat the oven to 350°F (175°C). In a baking dish, layer the sliced apples.
2. In a bowl, mix oats, almond flour, brown sugar, melted coconut oil, cinnamon, and salt until crumbly.
3. Sprinkle the mixture over the apples.
4. Bake for 30-35 minutes until the topping is golden brown and the apples are tender.

Peanut Butter Banana Ice Cream

Ingredients:

- 3 ripe bananas, sliced and frozen
- 1/2 cup peanut butter
- 1 tbsp maple syrup (optional)

Instructions:

1. In a food processor, blend the frozen banana slices until creamy.
2. Add peanut butter and maple syrup (if using) and blend until combined.
3. Serve immediately or freeze for a firmer texture.

Cacao Nib Energy Bites

Ingredients:

- 1 cup oats
- 1/2 cup almond butter
- 1/4 cup honey or maple syrup
- 1/4 cup cacao nibs
- 1/4 cup shredded coconut (optional)

Instructions:

1. In a bowl, combine oats, almond butter, honey (or maple syrup), cacao nibs, and shredded coconut.
2. Mix until well combined, then form into small balls.
3. Refrigerate for 30 minutes before serving.

Pumpkin Pie Bars

Ingredients:

- 1 cup almond flour
- 1/2 cup oats
- 1/4 cup coconut oil, melted
- 1/4 cup maple syrup
- 1 can (15 oz) pumpkin puree
- 1/2 cup coconut milk
- 1/2 cup maple syrup
- 2 tsp pumpkin pie spice
- 1 tsp vanilla extract

Instructions:

1. Preheat the oven to 350°F (175°C) and grease an 8x8-inch baking pan.
2. In a bowl, mix almond flour, oats, melted coconut oil, and maple syrup. Press into the bottom of the prepared pan.
3. In another bowl, combine pumpkin puree, coconut milk, maple syrup, pumpkin pie spice, and vanilla extract. Pour over the crust.
4. Bake for 30-35 minutes until set. Allow to cool before cutting into bars.

Chocolate Avocado Brownies

Ingredients:

- 1 ripe avocado, mashed
- 1/2 cup cocoa powder
- 1/2 cup almond flour
- 1/2 cup maple syrup
- 1/4 cup coconut oil, melted
- 1 tsp vanilla extract
- 1/2 tsp baking soda

Instructions:

1. Preheat the oven to 350°F (175°C) and grease an 8x8-inch baking pan.
2. In a bowl, mix mashed avocado, cocoa powder, almond flour, maple syrup, melted coconut oil, vanilla extract, and baking soda until well combined.
3. Pour the batter into the prepared pan and bake for 20-25 minutes.
4. Let cool before cutting into squares.

Peach Crumble

Ingredients:

- 4 cups sliced peaches (fresh or frozen)
- 1/2 cup almond flour
- 1/2 cup oats
- 1/4 cup brown sugar
- 1/4 cup coconut oil, melted
- 1 tsp cinnamon
- Pinch of salt

Instructions:

1. Preheat the oven to 350°F (175°C) and grease a baking dish.
2. In a bowl, mix sliced peaches with cinnamon and a pinch of salt, then pour into the baking dish.
3. In another bowl, combine almond flour, oats, brown sugar, and melted coconut oil. Mix until crumbly.
4. Sprinkle the topping over the peaches.
5. Bake for 25-30 minutes until the topping is golden and the peaches are bubbly.

Vegan Lemon Bars

Ingredients:

- 1 cup almond flour
- 1/4 cup coconut oil, melted
- 1/4 cup maple syrup
- 1/2 cup lemon juice
- 1/4 cup coconut milk
- 1/4 cup cornstarch
- 1 tsp vanilla extract

Instructions:

1. Preheat the oven to 350°F (175°C) and grease an 8x8-inch baking pan.
2. In a bowl, mix almond flour, melted coconut oil, and maple syrup until well combined. Press into the bottom of the pan.
3. In another bowl, whisk together lemon juice, coconut milk, cornstarch, and vanilla extract until smooth.
4. Pour the filling over the crust and bake for 25-30 minutes until set.
5. Let cool before cutting into bars.

Date and Nut Energy Balls

Ingredients:

- 1 cup dates, pitted
- 1/2 cup almonds or walnuts
- 1/4 cup shredded coconut
- 1 tbsp chia seeds (optional)
- Pinch of salt

Instructions:

1. In a food processor, combine dates, nuts, shredded coconut, chia seeds, and salt. Blend until a sticky dough forms.
2. Roll the mixture into small balls and place on a tray.
3. Refrigerate for at least 30 minutes before serving.

Dairy-Free Chocolate Cake

Ingredients:

- 1 1/2 cups almond flour
- 1/2 cup cocoa powder
- 1/2 cup maple syrup
- 1/4 cup coconut oil, melted
- 1/2 cup almond milk
- 1 tsp baking soda
- 1 tsp vanilla extract

Instructions:

1. Preheat the oven to 350°F (175°C) and grease an 8-inch round cake pan.
2. In a bowl, mix almond flour, cocoa powder, baking soda, and salt.
3. In another bowl, whisk together maple syrup, melted coconut oil, almond milk, and vanilla extract.
4. Combine wet and dry ingredients and pour into the prepared pan.
5. Bake for 25-30 minutes until a toothpick comes out clean. Let cool before serving.

Mango Coconut Sticky Rice

Ingredients:

- 1 cup sticky rice (glutinous rice)
- 1 cup coconut milk
- 1/4 cup sugar
- 1 ripe mango, sliced
- Pinch of salt

Instructions:

1. Rinse the sticky rice until the water runs clear, then soak for 4 hours or overnight.
2. Steam the soaked rice for 20-25 minutes until cooked.
3. In a saucepan, heat coconut milk, sugar, and salt until dissolved.
4. Once the rice is done, mix with the coconut milk mixture. Let sit for 30 minutes.
5. Serve with sliced mango on top.

Dairy-Free Chocolate Bark

Ingredients:

- 1 cup dairy-free chocolate chips
- 1/2 cup nuts (almonds, walnuts, or hazelnuts)
- 1/4 cup dried fruit (cranberries, raisins, or apricots)

Instructions:

1. Melt the chocolate chips in a microwave or double boiler until smooth.
2. Stir in nuts and dried fruit.
3. Pour the mixture onto a parchment-lined baking sheet and spread evenly.
4. Refrigerate until set, then break into pieces.

Lemon Coconut Macaroons

Ingredients:

- 2 cups shredded coconut
- 1/2 cup almond flour
- 1/3 cup maple syrup
- 1/4 cup lemon juice
- 1 tsp vanilla extract

Instructions:

1. Preheat the oven to 325°F (160°C) and line a baking sheet with parchment paper.
2. In a bowl, combine shredded coconut, almond flour, maple syrup, lemon juice, and vanilla extract.
3. Drop spoonfuls of the mixture onto the baking sheet.
4. Bake for 15-20 minutes until golden brown. Let cool before serving.

Coconut Flour Pancakes

Ingredients:

- 1/4 cup coconut flour
- 1/4 cup almond milk
- 2 eggs
- 1 tbsp coconut oil, melted
- 1 tsp baking powder
- Pinch of salt

Instructions:

1. In a bowl, mix coconut flour, baking powder, and salt.
2. In another bowl, whisk together eggs, almond milk, and melted coconut oil.
3. Combine wet and dry ingredients until smooth.
4. Heat a skillet over medium heat and pour batter to form pancakes. Cook until bubbles form, then flip and cook until golden brown.
5. Serve with your favorite toppings.

Carrot Cake Muffins

Ingredients:

- 1 1/2 cups whole wheat flour
- 1 tsp baking soda
- 1 tsp cinnamon
- 1/2 tsp nutmeg
- 1/4 tsp salt
- 1/2 cup maple syrup
- 1/2 cup almond milk
- 1/3 cup coconut oil, melted
- 1 cup grated carrots
- 1/2 cup raisins (optional)

Instructions:

1. Preheat the oven to 350°F (175°C) and line a muffin tin with paper liners.
2. In a bowl, whisk together flour, baking soda, cinnamon, nutmeg, and salt.
3. In another bowl, mix maple syrup, almond milk, and melted coconut oil.
4. Combine wet and dry ingredients, then fold in grated carrots and raisins.
5. Divide the batter among the muffin cups and bake for 20-25 minutes until a toothpick comes out clean.

Dairy-Free Tiramisu

Ingredients:

- 1 cup strong brewed coffee, cooled
- 1/4 cup maple syrup
- 1/2 cup coconut cream
- 1/2 cup almond milk
- 1 tsp vanilla extract
- 1 package dairy-free ladyfingers
- Cocoa powder for dusting

Instructions:

1. In a bowl, mix coffee and maple syrup.
2. In another bowl, whisk together coconut cream, almond milk, and vanilla extract until smooth.
3. Dip each ladyfinger briefly in the coffee mixture and layer them in a dish.
4. Spread a layer of the coconut cream mixture over the ladyfingers. Repeat layers until all ingredients are used.
5. Dust with cocoa powder and refrigerate for at least 4 hours before serving.

Chocolate-Dipped Strawberries

Ingredients:

- 1 cup dairy-free chocolate chips
- 1 lb fresh strawberries, washed and dried

Instructions:

1. Melt the chocolate chips in a microwave-safe bowl or double boiler until smooth.
2. Dip each strawberry into the melted chocolate, allowing excess to drip off.
3. Place dipped strawberries on a parchment-lined baking sheet.
4. Refrigerate until the chocolate hardens, about 30 minutes.

Banana Coconut Muffins

Ingredients:

- 1 1/2 cups almond flour
- 1/2 cup mashed bananas (about 2 bananas)
- 1/4 cup maple syrup
- 1/4 cup coconut oil, melted
- 1/4 cup shredded coconut
- 1 tsp baking powder
- 1/2 tsp baking soda
- 1/4 tsp salt

Instructions:

1. Preheat the oven to 350°F (175°C) and line a muffin tin with paper liners.
2. In a bowl, combine almond flour, baking powder, baking soda, and salt.
3. In another bowl, mix mashed bananas, maple syrup, and melted coconut oil.
4. Combine wet and dry ingredients, then fold in shredded coconut.
5. Divide the batter among the muffin cups and bake for 20-25 minutes until a toothpick comes out clean.

Vegan Rice Crispy Treats

Ingredients:

- 3 cups brown rice cereal
- 1/4 cup coconut oil
- 1/4 cup maple syrup
- 1/2 tsp vanilla extract

Instructions:

1. In a saucepan, melt coconut oil and maple syrup over low heat. Stir in vanilla extract.
2. Remove from heat and mix in brown rice cereal until evenly coated.
3. Press the mixture into a greased 8x8-inch baking dish.
4. Let cool and set before cutting into squares.

Oatmeal Chocolate Chip Bars

Ingredients:

- 1 1/2 cups rolled oats
- 1/2 cup almond flour
- 1/2 cup maple syrup
- 1/4 cup coconut oil, melted
- 1/2 cup dairy-free chocolate chips
- 1/2 tsp vanilla extract
- 1/4 tsp salt

Instructions:

1. Preheat the oven to 350°F (175°C) and line an 8x8-inch baking dish with parchment paper.
2. In a bowl, mix rolled oats, almond flour, and salt.
3. In another bowl, whisk together maple syrup, melted coconut oil, and vanilla extract.
4. Combine wet and dry ingredients, then fold in chocolate chips.
5. Pour the batter into the prepared dish and bake for 20-25 minutes. Let cool before cutting into bars.

Raspberry Chia Seed Jam

Ingredients:

- 2 cups fresh or frozen raspberries
- 1/4 cup maple syrup
- 2 tbsp chia seeds
- 1 tbsp lemon juice

Instructions:

1. In a saucepan, combine raspberries and maple syrup over medium heat. Cook until raspberries break down.
2. Stir in chia seeds and lemon juice, then remove from heat.
3. Let the mixture cool and thicken for about 30 minutes before transferring to a jar.

Coconut Panna Cotta

Ingredients:

- 1 can (13.5 oz) coconut milk
- 1/4 cup maple syrup
- 1 tsp vanilla extract
- 1 tbsp agar-agar powder (or gelatin if not vegan)
- Pinch of salt

Instructions:

1. In a saucepan, combine coconut milk, maple syrup, vanilla extract, agar-agar, and salt.
2. Heat over medium heat, stirring until agar-agar dissolves.
3. Pour the mixture into ramekins and refrigerate until set, about 2-4 hours.
4. Serve chilled, topped with fresh fruit or chocolate sauce if desired.

Fruit Salad with Lime Dressing

Ingredients:

- 2 cups mixed fresh fruit (strawberries, blueberries, kiwi, pineapple, etc.)
- 1 lime, juiced
- 1 tbsp maple syrup (optional)
- Fresh mint leaves for garnish (optional)

Instructions:

1. In a large bowl, combine the mixed fresh fruit.
2. In a small bowl, whisk together lime juice and maple syrup until well combined.
3. Drizzle the lime dressing over the fruit and gently toss to coat.
4. Garnish with fresh mint leaves if desired and serve immediately.

Vegan Snickerdoodles

Ingredients:

- 1 cup coconut oil, solid
- 1 cup brown sugar
- 1/4 cup almond milk
- 1 tsp vanilla extract
- 2 cups all-purpose flour
- 1 tsp cream of tartar
- 1/2 tsp baking soda
- 1/4 tsp salt
- 2 tbsp cinnamon sugar (for rolling)

Instructions:

1. Preheat the oven to 350°F (175°C) and line a baking sheet with parchment paper.
2. In a large bowl, cream together solid coconut oil and brown sugar until fluffy.
3. Add almond milk and vanilla extract, mixing until smooth.
4. In another bowl, combine flour, cream of tartar, baking soda, and salt. Gradually add the dry mixture to the wet mixture, mixing until combined.
5. Roll the dough into balls, then roll each ball in cinnamon sugar.
6. Place on the prepared baking sheet and flatten slightly. Bake for 10-12 minutes until golden.

Chocolate Coconut Energy Bites

Ingredients:

- 1 cup rolled oats
- 1/2 cup almond butter
- 1/3 cup maple syrup
- 1/2 cup shredded coconut
- 1/4 cup dairy-free chocolate chips
- 1 tsp vanilla extract

Instructions:

1. In a large bowl, mix all ingredients until well combined.
2. Refrigerate the mixture for about 30 minutes to firm up.
3. Once chilled, scoop out tablespoon-sized portions and roll into balls.
4. Store in an airtight container in the refrigerator for up to a week.

Banana Split Bowl

Ingredients:

- 2 ripe bananas, halved lengthwise
- 1 cup dairy-free vanilla ice cream
- 1/2 cup fresh strawberries, sliced
- 1/2 cup pineapple chunks
- 1/4 cup dairy-free chocolate sauce
- Chopped nuts and cherries for topping (optional)

Instructions:

1. In a serving bowl, place the banana halves side by side.
2. Scoop the dairy-free vanilla ice cream and place it in the center of the banana.
3. Top with sliced strawberries, pineapple chunks, and drizzle with chocolate sauce.
4. Add chopped nuts and cherries on top if desired, then serve immediately.

Lemon Coconut Bars

Ingredients:

- 1 cup almond flour
- 1/4 cup coconut oil, melted
- 1/4 cup maple syrup
- 1/2 cup fresh lemon juice
- Zest of 1 lemon
- 1/4 cup shredded coconut
- 1/4 tsp salt

Instructions:

1. Preheat the oven to 350°F (175°C) and line an 8x8-inch baking dish with parchment paper.
2. In a bowl, mix almond flour, melted coconut oil, and maple syrup until combined.
3. Press the mixture into the bottom of the prepared baking dish.
4. In another bowl, whisk together lemon juice, lemon zest, shredded coconut, and salt. Pour over the crust.
5. Bake for 20-25 minutes until set and lightly golden. Let cool before cutting into squares.

Vegan Pumpkin Muffins

Ingredients:

- 1 cup canned pumpkin puree
- 1/2 cup maple syrup
- 1/4 cup almond milk
- 1/4 cup coconut oil, melted
- 1 1/2 cups all-purpose flour
- 1 tsp baking soda
- 1 tsp cinnamon
- 1/2 tsp nutmeg
- 1/4 tsp salt

Instructions:

1. Preheat the oven to 350°F (175°C) and line a muffin tin with paper liners.
2. In a bowl, mix together pumpkin puree, maple syrup, almond milk, and melted coconut oil until smooth.
3. In another bowl, combine flour, baking soda, cinnamon, nutmeg, and salt.
4. Gradually add dry ingredients to wet ingredients, mixing until just combined.
5. Divide the batter among the muffin cups and bake for 20-25 minutes until a toothpick comes out clean.

Chocolate Chip Blondies

Ingredients:

- 1 cup almond flour
- 1/2 cup coconut sugar
- 1/4 cup almond butter
- 1/4 cup coconut oil, melted
- 1/4 cup almond milk
- 1 tsp vanilla extract
- 1/2 tsp baking powder
- 1/4 tsp salt
- 1/2 cup dairy-free chocolate chips

Instructions:

1. Preheat the oven to 350°F (175°C) and line an 8x8-inch baking dish with parchment paper.
2. In a bowl, mix almond flour, coconut sugar, almond butter, melted coconut oil, almond milk, and vanilla extract until smooth.
3. Add baking powder and salt, then mix until combined.
4. Fold in chocolate chips and pour the batter into the prepared dish.
5. Bake for 20-25 minutes until golden and set. Let cool before cutting into squares.

Peanut Butter Cups

Ingredients:

- 1 cup dairy-free chocolate chips
- 1/2 cup natural peanut butter
- 1/4 cup maple syrup
- 1/4 tsp salt

Instructions:

1. Line a muffin tin with paper liners.
2. Melt half the chocolate chips in a microwave-safe bowl until smooth.
3. Spoon a small amount of melted chocolate into the bottom of each liner and spread it up the sides.
4. In a bowl, mix peanut butter, maple syrup, and salt until smooth.
5. Fill each chocolate-coated cup with the peanut butter mixture, then top with the remaining melted chocolate.
6. Refrigerate until set, about 30 minutes.

Caramelized Pineapple

Ingredients:

- 1 ripe pineapple, peeled and sliced
- 1/4 cup coconut sugar
- 2 tbsp coconut oil
- 1 tsp vanilla extract
- 1/2 tsp cinnamon (optional)

Instructions:

1. Heat coconut oil in a large skillet over medium heat.
2. Add pineapple slices and sprinkle with coconut sugar, vanilla extract, and cinnamon if using.
3. Cook for about 3-4 minutes on each side until golden and caramelized.
4. Serve warm as a dessert or topping for pancakes, ice cream, or yogurt.

Vegan Chocolate Chip Pancakes

Ingredients:

- 1 cup all-purpose flour
- 2 tbsp coconut sugar
- 1 tsp baking powder
- 1/2 tsp baking soda
- 1/4 tsp salt
- 1 cup almond milk
- 2 tbsp coconut oil, melted
- 1 tsp vanilla extract
- 1/2 cup dairy-free chocolate chips

Instructions:

1. In a bowl, whisk together flour, coconut sugar, baking powder, baking soda, and salt.
2. In another bowl, mix almond milk, melted coconut oil, and vanilla extract.
3. Combine the wet ingredients with the dry ingredients until just mixed. Fold in chocolate chips.
4. Heat a non-stick skillet over medium heat and pour 1/4 cup of batter for each pancake. Cook until bubbles form, then flip and cook until golden brown.

Almond Joy Bites

Ingredients:

- 1 cup almond flour
- 1/2 cup shredded coconut
- 1/4 cup maple syrup
- 1/4 cup almond butter
- 1/2 tsp vanilla extract
- 1/4 cup dairy-free chocolate chips (for coating)

Instructions:

1. In a bowl, mix almond flour, shredded coconut, maple syrup, almond butter, and vanilla extract until well combined.
2. Form the mixture into small balls and place them on a parchment-lined baking sheet.
3. Freeze for 15-20 minutes until firm.
4. Melt the chocolate chips and dip each ball into the chocolate to coat. Return to the baking sheet and refrigerate until set.

Dairy-Free Key Lime Pie

Ingredients:

- 1 1/2 cups graham cracker crumbs
- 1/4 cup coconut oil, melted
- 1/4 cup maple syrup
- 1 cup coconut cream
- 1/2 cup fresh lime juice
- Zest of 2 limes
- 1/4 cup maple syrup (for filling)
- Pinch of salt

Instructions:

1. Preheat the oven to 350°F (175°C).
2. In a bowl, mix graham cracker crumbs, melted coconut oil, and maple syrup until combined. Press the mixture into the bottom of a pie dish to form the crust.
3. Bake for 10 minutes, then let cool.
4. In a blender, combine coconut cream, fresh lime juice, lime zest, maple syrup, and salt until smooth.
5. Pour the filling into the cooled crust and refrigerate for at least 4 hours to set.

Coconut Crème Brûlée

Ingredients:

- 1 can (13.5 oz) coconut milk
- 1/4 cup maple syrup
- 1 tsp vanilla extract
- 1 tbsp cornstarch
- Coconut sugar (for topping)

Instructions:

1. Preheat the oven to 325°F (160°C).
2. In a saucepan, heat coconut milk, maple syrup, and vanilla extract until warm.
3. In a small bowl, mix cornstarch with a little coconut milk to form a slurry, then add it back to the saucepan. Stir until thickened.
4. Pour the mixture into ramekins and bake in a water bath for 25-30 minutes until set.
5. Let cool, then refrigerate for at least 2 hours.
6. Before serving, sprinkle coconut sugar on top and caramelize with a kitchen torch until golden.

Chocolate Banana Bread

Ingredients:

- 3 ripe bananas, mashed
- 1/3 cup coconut oil, melted
- 1/2 cup maple syrup
- 1 tsp vanilla extract
- 1 cup all-purpose flour
- 1/2 cup cocoa powder
- 1 tsp baking soda
- 1/4 tsp salt
- 1/2 cup dairy-free chocolate chips

Instructions:

1. Preheat the oven to 350°F (175°C) and grease a loaf pan.
2. In a bowl, mix mashed bananas, melted coconut oil, maple syrup, and vanilla extract until smooth.
3. In another bowl, combine flour, cocoa powder, baking soda, and salt. Gradually add the dry mixture to the wet mixture.
4. Fold in chocolate chips and pour the batter into the prepared loaf pan.
5. Bake for 50-60 minutes until a toothpick comes out clean. Let cool before slicing.

Vegan Berry Parfait

Ingredients:

- 2 cups dairy-free yogurt
- 1 cup mixed fresh berries (strawberries, blueberries, raspberries)
- 1/2 cup granola
- 2 tbsp maple syrup (optional)

Instructions:

1. In a glass or bowl, layer dairy-free yogurt, mixed berries, and granola.
2. Repeat the layers until the glass is filled.
3. Drizzle with maple syrup if desired and serve immediately.

Dairy-Free Oatmeal Raisin Cookies

Ingredients:

- 1 cup rolled oats
- 1/2 cup almond flour
- 1/2 cup coconut sugar
- 1/4 cup coconut oil, melted
- 1/4 cup almond milk
- 1 tsp vanilla extract
- 1/2 tsp cinnamon
- 1/4 tsp salt
- 1/2 cup raisins

Instructions:

1. Preheat the oven to 350°F (175°C) and line a baking sheet with parchment paper.
2. In a bowl, mix oats, almond flour, coconut sugar, melted coconut oil, almond milk, vanilla extract, cinnamon, and salt until combined.
3. Fold in raisins.
4. Scoop tablespoon-sized portions onto the baking sheet and flatten slightly.
5. Bake for 10-12 minutes until golden. Let cool before serving.

Coconut Lime Pudding

Ingredients:

- 1 can (13.5 oz) coconut milk
- 1/4 cup maple syrup
- 1/4 cup cornstarch
- 1/4 cup fresh lime juice
- Zest of 1 lime
- 1/2 tsp vanilla extract
- Pinch of salt

Instructions:

1. In a medium saucepan, whisk together the coconut milk, maple syrup, and salt over medium heat.
2. In a separate bowl, mix the cornstarch with a few tablespoons of the coconut mixture to create a slurry.
3. Once the coconut mixture is warm, add the slurry and stir constantly until it thickens (about 5-7 minutes).
4. Remove from heat and stir in the lime juice, lime zest, and vanilla extract.
5. Pour the pudding into individual serving cups and refrigerate for at least 2 hours until set.

Chocolate Dipped Fruit

Ingredients:

- 1 cup dairy-free chocolate chips
- 1 tbsp coconut oil
- Assorted fresh fruits (strawberries, bananas, apple slices, pineapple chunks, etc.)

Instructions:

1. Line a baking sheet with parchment paper.
2. In a microwave-safe bowl, combine dairy-free chocolate chips and coconut oil. Microwave in 30-second intervals, stirring in between, until melted and smooth.
3. Dip each piece of fruit into the melted chocolate, allowing excess chocolate to drip off.
4. Place the chocolate-dipped fruit on the prepared baking sheet.
5. Optional: Sprinkle with sea salt or shredded coconut before the chocolate sets.
6. Refrigerate for about 30 minutes to allow the chocolate to harden before serving.

Enjoy your delightful treats!

Printed in the USA
CPSIA information can be obtained
at www.ICGtesting.com
LVHW080507291124
797659LV00009B/220